GENETICS

Please visit our web site at: **www.garethstevens.com**
For a free color catalog describing Gareth Stevens Publishing's list of high-quality books and multimedia programs, call 1-800-542-2595 (USA) or 1-800-387-3178 (Canada). Gareth Stevens Publishing's fax: (414) 332-3567.

Library of Congress Cataloging-in-Publication Data

Twisted.
        Genetics.
            p. cm. — (Discovery Channel school science. Universes large and small)
            Summary: Explores DNA, how it determines heredity, and some of the implications of recent genetic discoveries. Includes related activities.
            ISBN 0-8368-3370-8 (lib. bdg.)
            1. Genetics—Juvenile literature. [1. Genetics. 2. DNA.] I. Title. II. Series.
        QH437.5.T85   2003
        576.5—dc21   2003042494

This edition first published in 2004 by
Gareth Stevens Publishing
A World Almanac Education Group Company
330 West Olive Street, Suite 100
Milwaukee, WI 53212 USA

This U.S. edition copyright © 2004 by Gareth Stevens, Inc. First published in 1999 as *Twisted: The Genetics Files* by Discovery Enterprises, LLC, Bethesda, Maryland. © 1999 by Discovery Communications, Inc.

Further resources for students and educators available at www.discoveryschool.com

Designed by Bill SMITH STUDIO
Creative Director: Ron Leighton
Design: Eric Hoffsten, Jay Jaffe, Brian Kobberger, Nick Stone, Sonia Gauba
Photo Editor: Justine Price
Production Manager: Jeffrey Rutzky
Art Buyer: Lillie Caporlingua
Print consulting by Debbie Honig, Active Concepts

Gareth Stevens Editor: Betsy Rasmussen
Gareth Stevens Art Director: Tammy Gruenewald
Technical Advisor: Angela Pickart

Printed in the United States of America

1 2 3 4 5 6 7 8 9 07 06 05 04 03

Writers: Lew Parker, David Krasnow

Editors: Jackie Ball, Justine Ciovacco

Photographs: Cover, DNA, ©Will & Deni McIntyre/Photo Researchers, Inc.; p. 3, Dionne Quints, ©Corbis-Bettmann; p. 4-5, computer-generated DNA model, ©Ken Eward/ Science Source/Photo Researchers, Inc.; p. 9, Watson & Crick, ©A. Barrington Brown/Photo Researchers, Inc.; p. 10, Mendel, ©Corbis-Bettman; p. 11, McClintock, ©AP/Wide World Photos; p. 14, Dolly, ©AP/Wide World Photos; p. 16, True Blue, photo from John Graves (personal collection);

p. 18, X and Y chromosomes, ©Biophoto Associates/Photo Researchers, Inc.; p. 22, mosquito, ©Discovery; p. 24, fraternal twins, ©Aaron Haupt/Photo Researchers, Inc.; p. 27, Chang and Eng, ©Brown Brothers, Ltd.

Illustrations: P. 6-7, DNA rollercoaster, Bob Bruger; p. 13, imaginary animals, Jim Paillot; p. 25, cartoon, Bob Bruger; p. 26, triplets diagram, Chris Burke

Acknowledgements: p. 8-9, excerpts from THE DOUBLE HELIX by Gunther S. Stent (ed.). ©1980 by W.W. Norton & Company, Inc.; p. 16, background information for True Blue, http://wsrv.clas.virginia.edu/~rjh9u/fugpednew.html

CONTENTS

GENETICS

How come you're not a frog? Good question. After all, when a human sperm and egg joined to form a cell with your name on it, they were going through the same process as their froggy counterparts. So how did a fertilized egg "know" how to grow into you?

In the 1700s, someone using a very primitive microscope—far less accurate than the one in your classroom—believed he saw a tiny person in the head of a sperm cell. He called this minuscule person a *homunculus* and believed that it would grow in the womb into a human. Now we know that a twisted molecule called DNA determines heredity, or how characteristics are passed from parents to offspring. Discoveries in this aspect of biology, called genetics, come fast and furious. In *GENETICS*, Discovery Channel lets you explore DNA and the staggering implications new genetic discoveries are having on your life and world.

Five of a kind. See page 26.

Genetics

What makes a human a human, an aardvark an aardvark, and a cabbage a cabbage? It ▒▒▒▒ to do with a long, thin, spiral-shaped molecule called DNA—short for deoxyribonucleic acid—contained in all living things. Including you, of course. You have these molecules in your body, in every c▒▒ Within these skinny, twisted strands are sets of instructions called genes. You have about thirty to forty thousand of them. Genes are found in pairs, one inherited from your mom and one from your dad. Every gene is a tiny blueprint, with instructions passed by your parents to tell your cells exactly how to create a unique you.

DNA–A long, twisted molecule usually found only in the nucleus and to a lesser extent in some organelles of every cell. DNA contains information in the form of genes, and this information directs all cell activities.

DOUBLE HELIX–The structure of DNA. A helix is a strand that is coiled like a Slinky™. A double helix is like two of these toys wrapped around each other. Or imagine a ladder, then imagine it twisted at both ends in opposite directions. The long edges of the ladder twist around each other to form a double helix.

BACKBONE–If you imagine DNA as a twisted ladder, then the two long sides of the ladder are its backbones. They're made of repeating units of deoxyribose sugar and a phosphate group.

RNA–Short for ribonucleic acid. It differs in three ways from DNA:
❶ RNA has only one strand—one long side of a ladder—not two
❷ RNA has ribose as its backbone sugar, not deoxyribose
❸ RNA contains the nitrogenous base uracil, not the thymine of DNA

BASE PAIRS–Staying with the twisted ladder idea, the base pairs are the steps of the ladder. Each step is made up of two nitrogenous (nitrogen-containing) bases. There are four bases: adenine (A), thymine (T), guanine (G), and cytosine (C). Adenine always pairs with thymine, and guanine always pairs with cytosine.

GENE–A section of DNA with a specific sequence of nitrogenous bases. This sequence is the code that directs the manufacture of a protein or part of a protein. And those proteins will make up your body tissues and perform various functions in your body.

Nitrogenous Bases

Phosphate Groups

Deoxyribose Sugar Groups

Repeating units of these make up a DNA molecule's backbones.

Chain of Events DNA makes RNA makes proteins. DNA contains the genetic code that allows it to make different kinds of RNA. One kind of RNA migrates out of the nucleus to ribosomes, where it directs the synthesis of proteins. Proteins do the work of the cell. They are a major component of a cell's structure, and they are the enzymes that allow the cell's chemical reactions to occur.

Ride the Wild Helix

This is one weird carnival you've stumbled into. And what is that barker shouting? "Step right up! Shrink right down! You have got to be microscopic to ride inside the Wild Helix. Ride it if you dare! Hitch a ride on the Spiral Staircase, the Thread of Life!"

Because you are actually inside a cell's nucleus, you are very, very, very small. Small enough to climb into one of the cars attached to one edge of what looks like a twisted ladder, or the tracks of a roller coaster. The Wild Helix turns out to be a very long DNA molecule, made up of different parts. The most obvious pieces are the long strand that is a track for your car and another strand running parallel to it. These strands are the backbones of a DNA molecule, and they are made of sugar and phosphate units.

You look down and notice that the strand you are on is connected to the other one by a series of short bases. If this were a roller coaster, these would be the rail ties. But this is no roller coaster! There are four different kinds of nitrogen-containing bases, each stamped with a letter. A is for adenine, G is for guanine, T is for thymine, and C is for cytosine.

As you zoom along the helix, you notice that the bases are arranged in a precise way. Bases in the first strand pair directly with the bases in the other strand. A is always paired with T, and C is always paired with G. You glance at the bases as you go by, and you read the sequence of letters in the bases connecting the two strands:

A-G-T-G-C-A-C-G-T

T-C-A-C-G-T-G-C-A

It looks like a code of some kind. And it is—the cell will know how to translate it, even if you don't.

Now you're whipping down the DNA ladder, and

the ride is getting choppy. The two strands start pulling apart. Stay to the left! That's the way. The Wild Helix is always in motion, always combining and splitting, splitting and combining. Suddenly, another strand appears right next to you. It's a lot smaller than the DNA molecule you're on. It turns out to be an RNA molecule, equipped to pick up and deliver a message. DNA stands for deoxyribonucleic acid, while RNA stands for ribonucleic acid. Call it "messenger RNA" or "mRNA" for short.

Click! With a jolt, a strand of mRNA attaches to a section of the DNA molecule right near your car. The bases on your strand attach to the matching bases on the mRNA. It's copying that code you saw earlier. You notice that mRNA's code is slightly different from the DNA's, though. Instead of the T (thymine) base, the RNA uses U, for uracil. But the strands line up just the same.

DNA strand	T-C-A-C-G-T-G-C-A
messenger RNA	A-G-U-G-C-A-C-G-U

As it finishes copying, a long strand of mRNA begins breaking off. Suddenly, your car flies off the DNA track. Your knuckles turn white as your car lands with a bump on the mRNA strand. It starts floating away, right toward the wall of the nucleus. Watch out! You're going to hit!

You duck. With a popping sound, the mRNA has squeezed through one of the pores of the nucleus. You've never felt so relieved. You made it through the nucleic membrane and you're still in one piece.

Now everything slows down. You're floating slowly through the cell's liquid cytoplasm. You travel past other cell structures, coming to a stop at a ribosome. This is the cell's protein factory, where mRNA will deliver its message. The ribosome will use the code to assemble amino acids into proteins. Proteins will make up your body tissues and will communicate with organs all over the body. You've reached your destination safely, having experienced the ride of a lifetime!

Activity

ALONG FOR THE RIDE Every person carries about *100 billion miles* (160 billion km) of DNA in his or her body. Do some research on the diameter of our Solar System. If you could stretch out all of the DNA into one strand, how far could you ride around the Solar System? How many times could you visit certain planets?

Birth of a Molecule

Naples, Italy, 1953

James Watson was a young American recently out of graduate school and excited to be among the famous scientists of his day. The components of the DNA molecule (a sugar, a phosphate, and a nitrogen base) were known. But its structure remained a mystery. So did its method of copying itself to pass along to other cells. No microscope capable of viewing individual molecules existed at the time. In the end, it was brain work and deduction that yielded answers, as Watson describes below (in black type).

It was Maurice Wilkins who first excited me about X-ray work on DNA. This happened at Naples when a small scientific meeting was held on the structures of the large molecules found in living cells. . . . I was in Europe on a postdoctoral fellowship [a grant awarded to a recent graduate] to learn its biochemistry. My interest in DNA had grown out of a desire, first picked up while a senior in college, to learn what the gene was. . . . It was my hope that the gene might be solved without my learning any chemistry. This wish arose from laziness since, as an undergraduate at the University of Chicago, I was principally interested in birds and managed to avoid taking any chemistry or physics courses which looked of even medium difficulty. Briefly the Indiana biochemists encouraged me to learn some organic chemistry, but after I used a bunsen burner to warm up some benzene, I was relieved from further true chemistry. It was safer to turn out an uneducated Ph.D. than to risk another explosion.

My Ph.D. supervisor, the Italian-trained microbiologist Salvador Luria, studied phages [a kind of virus] with the hope that they would eventually learn how the genes controlled cellular heredity. . . . Deep down he knew that it is impossible to describe the behavior of something when you don't know what it is. Thus, knowing he could never bring himself to study chemistry, Luria felt that the wisest course was to send me, his first serious student, to a chemist.

At the Cavendish Laboratory of Cambridge University, Watson met Francis Crick, a physicist who had begun to study biological molecules. Brilliant but sometimes difficult, Crick had more ideas than he knew what to do with.

Francis . . . occasionally did experiments but more often was immersed in the theories for solving protein structures. Often he came up with something novel, would become enormously excited, and immediately tell it to anyone who would listen. A day or so later he would realize that his theory did not work and return to experiments, until boredom generated a new attack on theory. . . . He talked louder and faster than anyone else and, when he laughed, his location within the Cavendish was obvious.

Watson's ideas about DNA immediately stirred Crick's interest. The two hit it off and became a team; a colleague referred to them as "scientific clowns." They shortly discovered that Linus Pauling, the most famous and brilliant chemist of their day, was also studying the molecule at his laboratory in Pasadena, California. For Pauling, mapping the DNA structure would be one more achievement—maybe his biggest. For the two young, unknown scientists, it would make them, overnight, giants in their field. Basing their theory on x-ray photos colleagues Maurice Wilkins and Rosalind Franklin had taken, Watson and Crick suspected the DNA was a helix, a spiral. But did it have one strand or more? How were the nitrogen bases arranged? Did they point toward the inside or the outside of the spiral?

Generally, it was late in the evening after I got back to my rooms that I tried to puzzle out the mystery of the bases. . . . So I could be sure that I had the correct structures . . . I drew tiny pictures of the bases on sheets of Cavendish notepaper. My aim was somehow to arrange the centrally located bases in such a way that the backbones on the outside were completely regular—that is, giving the sugar-phosphate groups of each nucleotide identical three-dimensional configurations. But each time I tried to come up with a solution I ran into the obstacle that the four bases each had quite a different shape. . . . Thus, unless some very special trick existed, randomly twisting two polynucleotide chains around one another should result in a big mess. In some places the bigger bases must touch each other, while in other regions, where smaller bases would lie opposite each other, there must exist a gap or else their backbone regions must buckle in.

Watson and Crick headed down a number of wrong avenues. One of these was that each of the four nitrogen bases would bond with another of the same kind. But one day everything changed.

I spent the rest of the afternoon cutting accurate representations of the bases out of stiff cardboard. When I got to our still empty office the following morning, I quickly cleared away the papers from my desk top so that I would have a large, flat surface on which to form pairs of bases held together by hydrogen bonds. Though I initially went back to my like-with-like prejudices, I saw all too well that they led nowhere.

Suddenly I became aware that an adenine-thymine pair held together by two hydrogen bonds was identical in shape to a guanine-cytosine pair. . . . No fudging was required. Even more exciting, this type of double-helix suggested a replication [copying] scheme. . . . Given the base sequence of one chain, the sequence of its partner was automatically determined. Upon his arrival Francis did not get more than halfway through the door before I let loose that the answer to everything was in our hands. However, we both knew that we would not be home until a complete model was built in which all the stereochemical contacts were satisfactory. There was also the obvious fact

the implications of its existence were far too important to risk crying wolf. Thus I felt slightly queasy when at lunch Francis winged into the Eagle to tell everyone within hearing distance that we had found the secret of life.

James Watson (above left) was only twenty-five years old at the time of the discovery in 1953. He, Crick (above right), and Maurice Wilkins shared the Nobel Prize for it in 1962. Some considered it bad judgment that Rosalind Franklin, who had died very young in 1958, was not included in the Prize. Watson wrote about the discovery in *The Double Helix* in 1968, the source of the excerpts you've just read. The book recounts what may be the most important discovery in biology in this century. Watson also tells about the rivalry between scientists to discover it first.

Activity

BUILD YOUR OWN DNA Watson and Crick borrowed a method from Linus Pauling in trying to solve their problem. They had models of all the elements known to be in DNA built and "played" with them to figure out how the molecule would best fit together. Based on photographs in this book or other reference sources, use clay, Styrofoam, cardboard, or other materials to create your own model of the double helix in three dimensions.

Genetic Evolution

How did we get from the homunculus, the microscopic person inside a sperm cell, to DNA? It's only in the last 135 years that modern genetics has taken shape. That's not to say that the ideas behind genetics were entirely new. Even in prehistoric times, agricultural peoples practiced breeding of plants (such as wheat) to influence how the offspring turned out (wheat with bigger and better grains). Breeding of animals isn't all that different: Encourage two big, strong horses to mate, and there's a good chance that their foal will also be a big, strong horse—maybe even bigger and stronger than the parents. Over time, the practice of breeding led to our discovery of the laws of heredity and our newest field of study—genetic engineering.

1866

In the garden of the Austrian monastery where he lived and worked, Gregor Mendel wondered how traits are inherited from one pea plant to the next. He began conducting his own experiments by breeding the plants selectively and observing the results. The result: the basic laws of heredity that underlie modern genetics.

1882

Walther Flemming, a German scientist, examined salamander cells under a microscope. He saw threads in the nucleus of the cells which seemed to be dividing. These threads were later identified as chromosomes.

1901–1905

Dutch botanist Hugo de Vries published a study of gene mutation in plants. The mutation theory eventually explained how some diseases start.

A puzzle had been solved: Until then, there had been considerable debate about whether sex was an inherited trait or determined as an embryo developed in the womb. Research by Nettie Stevens showed that the chromosomes called X and Y (for their shapes) determine the sex of an individual. Women have two X chromosomes (XX); men have one X and one Y chromosome (XY). If you get your father's X chromosome, you're a girl; if you get his Y, you're a boy.

1909

By researching fruit flies, Thomas Hunt Morgan discovered that some genes are "sex linked"—that is, associated with the chromosome that determines sex. Morgan found that all white-eyed fruit flies are male. He reasoned that the fruit fly's gene for colored eyes was on the sex chromosome that only females carry. This was the first time that anyone had placed a specific gene on a specific chromosome.

1944

Scientists Oswald Avery, Colin MacLeod, and Maclyn McCarty examined a bacterium called *Pneumococcus*. They showed that traits can be transmitted from one cell to another by DNA molecules. This means that the DNA molecule is the basis of inherited characteristics. Experimenting with multicolored corn, Barbara McClintock demonstrated that the place of a gene on a DNA strand is not permanently fixed; "jumping genes" can change places. Her findings offered a key to understanding how a species evolves into another. But her theory was so radical that it was ignored by most other scientists.

1953

In what may be the key moment for twentieth-century biology, two scientists, James Watson and Francis Crick, discovered the structure of DNA. The DNA molecule looks like a ladder twisted to form a spiral, a form known as the double helix. Watson and Crick also learned how DNA reproduces itself.

1964

A team of scientists, including Charles Yanofsky, proved that a sequence of nitro-genous bases in DNA matches the sequence of amino acids in proteins. Amino acids are the simple chemical building blocks from which long proteins are made up. This was the first demonstration of how DNA directs the cell in creating proteins.

1973

Experiments by Stanley Cohen and Herbert Boyer showed that genes can be spliced —cut and pasted— from the DNA of one organism to another. The field of genetic engineering was born.

1990–1992

Mary Claire King, a scientist at the University of California, analyzed chromosomes from women whose family members had cancer. She found a gene on chromosome 17 that causes the inherited form of breast cancer.

Daniel Cohen and a team of international researchers produced a map of genetic markers on all twenty-three human chromosome pairs. These genetic markers are used in human genetic research to study families

1997–1998

Cloning is the rage. Ian Wilmut of the Roslin Institute in Scotland announces that a sheep named Dolly had been cloned from the cell of an adult female sheep. University of Hawaii scientists announced that they cloned a mouse, and then used the clone to clone more mice. Scientists at Kinki University in Japan said that they had cloned eight identical calves from the cells of one adult cow.

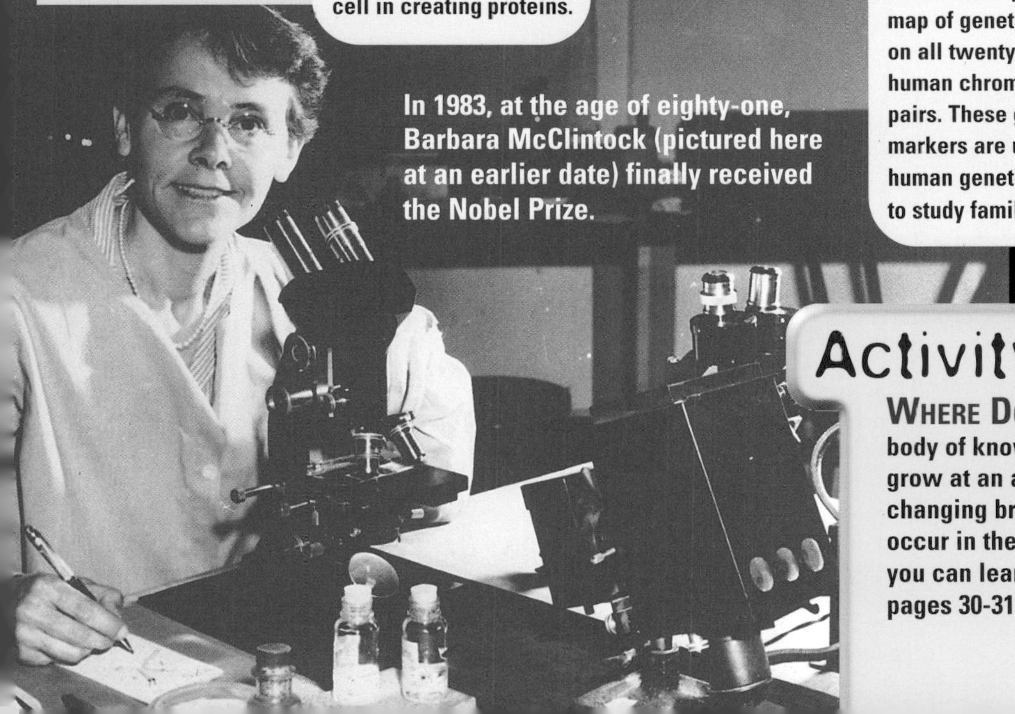

In 1983, at the age of eighty-one, Barbara McClintock (pictured here at an earlier date) finally received the Nobel Prize.

Activity

WHERE DO WE GO FROM HERE? Our body of knowledge of genetics continues to grow at an amazing speed. Fill in three world-changing breakthroughs in genetics that will occur in the next twenty years or so. For ideas, you can learn about genetic engineering on pages 30-31. Or use only your imagination.

11

True Gene-ius

Few scientists have had the impact on their field that Gregor Mendel had on genetics. Yet, he was a monk before he became a scientist. He joined the Augustinian monastery in the city now known as Brno. His talents and interests soon became clear to his superiors, and Mendel gladly went to the University of Vienna to receive training in math and science. He returned to teach these subjects at the monastery.

As a scientist, Mendel posed a question he found compelling: Why do the same kinds of plants show different traits? To begin answering this question, Mendel began experiments with garden peas in 1856. Why the pea? The monks raised twenty-two varieties, so there were plenty of different traits to experiment with. The pea grew quickly, so Mendel's experiments could take many generations into account quickly. And after observing and recording his results, he could snack on his research subjects, which he certainly couldn't have done with humans.

Mendel picked seven pea characteristics to study. Each characteristic came with just two traits: plant height (tall or short), seed color (green or yellow), seed-coat color (gray or white), pod shape (full or wrinkled), pod color (green or yellow), and flower distribution (along length or at the end of stem). Unlike many obvious human characteristics, most of these pea characteristics showed what is called discontinuous variation: tall *or* short, green *or* yellow, smooth *or* wrinkled, with no in-betweens. That makes peas easier for a geneticist to study than continuous variation (such as *how tall, what shade* of brown hair, and so on).

Mendel worked meticulously. He kept careful records of the plants that were crossed and the offspring produced. When he crossed short plants with other short plants, the offspring were always short. But when he crossed tall plants with other tall plants, he found that some tall plants produced tall offspring, while others produced both tall and short offspring.

This was puzzling. Sitting in front of his notes, chewing on a tough pea pod, Mendel came up with another experiment. He crossed tall plants that had produced only tall offspring with short plants that had produced only short offspring. The results: In the first generation (called F1), all the plants were tall. Yet, when the tall F1 plants were crossed, some of the second generation (F2) were short. The tall F1 plants must have had a capacity for shortness; they didn't show it, but they passed it onto their offspring.

In 1866, Mendel published a paper entitled "Experiments in Plant Hybridization." After many experiments, Mendel formulated three laws of genetics. They are still the guiding ideas of inheritance today.

Principle of Segregation: Every single trait is the result of a pair of "factors," now known as genes. The pair separates, or segregates, when sex cells (the female's egg and the male's sperm) form. Therefore, a sperm or egg will contain a factor either for tallness or shortness—not both.

Principle of Independent Assortment: Genes for different traits segregate independently of one another during the formation of sex cells, so that genes are inherited independently of each other. That is, the gene for tallness may be inherited with green or yellow seeds, smooth or wrinkled pods.

Principle of Dominance: An organism receives two genes for each trait, one gene from each parent. Only one gene of each pair is expressed. A dominant gene hides the other, or prevents it from being expressed. That's why two tall pea plants could still have short offspring. The parents had the recessive gene for shortness, which was "hidden" by the dominant gene for tallness.

Mendel's work is all the more impressive in that it was done a century before the DNA molecule was characterized. But at the time, no one, including Mendel himself, thought of him as a great scientist.

Hip to Be Square

An English geneticist named Reginald Punnett developed a convenient way to show the inheritance of a particular trait. Known as the Punnett square, this is how it works. Let's imagine creatures called clackatoids. Most clackatoids are purple, but a few are orange. In clackatoids, purple is the dominant gene for color. A geneticist would indicate the purple gene with a capital "P" and the orange gene with a lowercase "p."

An orange clackatoid cannot have a purple gene because its genetic makeup, or "genotype," for color is "pp," or two recessive genes for orange. Its offspring would inherit a "p" no matter what. A purple clackatoid, on the other hand, might have a color genotype of "PP" or "Pp," but you couldn't tell the difference just by looking at it, because in either case, the clackatoid is purple. In this case, the purple clackatoid's genotype is "Pp."

What would happen if these two clackatoids had offspring? What colors would they be? The Punnett square will help indicate all possible genotypes for the baby clackatoids. The color genes for the orange clackatoid's sex cells are shown on top of the box. Those of the purple clackatoid run on the left side. The genotypes inside the box indicate the four possible combinations for their offspring. Any baby with a genotype that includes a "P" will be purple, while any with *both* "p" genes will be orange.

| | Orange Clackatoid | |
	p	p
P	Pp	Pp
p	pp	pp

Purple Clackatoid

Hello, Dolly

Ladies and gentlemen, thank you for joining me today. Before her death in 2003, Dolly the sheep graciously consented to the following interview. Her birth in 1996 was quite possibly the biggest scientific news of the 1990s. She was, beyond a shadow of a doubt, the most famous sheep on planet Earth. You've probably heard a lot about her, but this was her first and only opportunity to explain herself to the media. Here're Dolly's words.

Q: Thanks for joining us, Dolly. Your birth was the focus of enormous media attention back in 1997. How was that for you?

A: Well, as you can imagine, it was a bit overwhelming for a young ewe from Scotland. But Dr. Ian Wilmut and the scientists at Roslin Institute were very kind, and I've had a lot of support.

Q: Dr. Wilmut is . . . ?

A: My father.

Q: Your father!?

A: Oh, I didn't mean it literally! But I've always thought of him as my father.

Q: I guess you and your ram father weren't close.

A: It's not like that. I don't have a father at all.

Q: Uh, Dolly, how is that possible?

A: I'm a clone. Dr. Wilmut and his team cloned me from my mother.

Q: Oh, I see. Yes, my daughter looks just like her mother, too. Spitting image. Same hair, eyes, mouth, way of standing, even the sound of her voice. It's uncanny.

A: Maybe you don't understand. Your daughter may have a lot of her mother's traits, but she has your genes as well. My mother and I are genetically identical. That's why I'm so famous. It was the first time that an adult mammal was cloned.

Q: The first clone ever?

A: Oh, no. The first clone from an adult mammal. Other living things are clones. Quite a few plants, in fact. Seedless grapes are clones. Human identical twins are clones of one another. In 1952, scientists created the first clones. They used cells from frog embryos to clone several frogs. Artificial twins, in other words.

Q: Who could tell? Sheep look pretty much alike to me.

A: I beg your pardon! A Finn Dorset sheep and a Scottish Blackface are as different from one another as any two humans.

Q: Oh, I'm sorry. No offense intended! You and your mother, though, must look exactly alike. You must think alike, too. You must have exactly the same personality. Talk about being a chip off the old block.

A: We're not as alike as you might guess. My development—and this is true of any animal, sheep as well as humans—was affected in lots of ways that weren't written in my genes. The exact conditions in the womb, the amount of nutrition I receive, the amount of exercise I get, a childhood illness that could stunt the growth a bit—all these things make clones slightly different. Take a look at human identical twins if you don't believe me—you can almost always find differences in them even though their DNA is identical. And of course our minds and personalities are quite different, because learning and experience play a huge role in what happens upstairs.

Q: That's fascinating. I'm still a little puzzled by your not having a father. Aren't you missing some, what do you call them, chromosomes?

A: I have the normal number. The Roslin scientists took udder cells from my mother and placed them in the egg cell of another sheep. That cell was placed in the uterus of a third sheep. Then I developed in the womb like any sheep embryo.

Q: Why didn't they just use egg cells?

A: Egg cells only have half the number of chromosomes of other cells. They need another half-set of chromosomes, which comes from sperm cells, to start producing a lamb. So scientists "tricked" an egg cell into thinking it had been fertilized.

Q: Quite an achievement. And you're quite a sheep, Dolly. Yet some people were quite worried when you were cloned.

A: Yes, a lot of the controversy focused on the fact that sheep and humans aren't that different, in evolutionary terms. A grape and a frog are one thing, but as soon as a large mammal like myself was cloned, people understood that human cloning was a possibility. And that has huge implications. I'm not going to go there. You should talk to some humans about that.

Q: Of course. One last question, and I hope this isn't too sensitive for you. Quite a few attempts to clone mammals have failed. Many of the small clones die in the uterus, and sometimes the animals bearing the cloned embryos have died as well. Young clones who appear to be healthy have died suddenly from birth defects. Can you shed any light on the problems?

A: Scientists aren't sure what has gone wrong with so many clone attempts. It's possible that it has to do with gene imprinting. Imprinting is a phenomenon where certain genes only work if inherited from the mother, while other genes only work if inherited from the father. Obviously, a clone could throw off such a system and could result in problems with development. Research to address these problems will be important if cloning becomes more common.

Q: Dolly, it's really been a pleasure having you and most enlightening, too. Best of luck.

DOLLY: THE SIX-STEP PLAN

1. A cell is taken from the udder of Sheep Number 1 (a Finn Dorset ewe). The cell is "starved" for five days, which tricks the cell into stopping its normal cycle of growth, so it doesn't divide.

2. An egg is taken from Sheep Number 2. The nucleus is removed.

3. Chromosomes are taken from the udder cell of Sheep Number 1 and inserted into the empty egg cell nucleus of Sheep Number 2.

4. The cell is given an electrical shock to start development.

5. The embryo is transplanted into the uterus of Sheep Number 3 (a Scottish Blackface ewe).

6. The embryo develops in the womb. Dolly is born as though she were Number 3's daughter. Maybe she is; but she shares none of her traits. She is the clone of Number 1.

True Blue

Lorenzo Dow Fugate and his wife, Eleanor, in the early 1900s. Color photography wasn't available back then, but if it had been, you might notice a bluish tint to Lorenzo's skin. He was a descendant of the so-called "blue Fugates."

Way back in 1962, Crayola™ changed the name of one of its popular crayon colors from "flesh" to "peach," recognizing that not everyone's skin is the same color. That is certainly true, but one color that people in the company probably never considered for a skin color was blue. Yes, it's true—blue.

In 1820, a French orphan named Martin Fugate and his wife, Elizabeth Smith, began a life together on the banks of Troublesome Creek in eastern Kentucky. They had eight children, four of whom were born with blue skin. That wasn't as much of a surprise as you might imagine, because Martin was also blue.

Because the Fugate offspring lived in a modest, isolated part of the country without any roads, they ended up marrying those who lived closest to them. Fugate off-spring married the members of the Smith, Combs, Ritchie, and Stacy families. They also married other Fugates, sometimes even first cousins. More than one hundred years later, the blue-skinned trait is still being passed on in these families.

It's in the Genes

The first medical professional to come in contact with two of the descendants, Patrick and Rachel Ritchie, was Dr. Madison Cawein, a hematologist from the University of Kentucky. In the 1960s, he had trouble defining just what gave them their blue color until he saw a study on methemoglobinemia (meth E mo globe in E mia) among some Alaskan Eskimo and Native American families. Methemo-globinemia is a rare blood disorder that creates excessive amounts of methemoglobin in the blood.

Methemoglobin is a blue form of the red hemoglobin that carries oxygen. The blood in many of the descendants of the Fugates had accumulated so much of the blue molecule that it overwhelmed the red color in normal hemoglobin. That red color under the skin helps make most Caucasians look pink-ish, so you can imagine that a lot of blue methemoglobin would make people look bluish.

In the average person, hemoglo-bin is converted to methemoglobin at a very slow rate. An enzyme called diaphorase converts methe-moglobin back to hemoglobin. The people with blue skin seem to have no diaphorase in their red blood cells. Their bluish complex-ion may or may not be obvious normally, but the blue in their skin usually darkens when they are cold, sick, or under stress.

The exact skin color of the early

Fugates who inherited the gene from both sides of their family isn't known, though family and local legend notes that a few had a blue coloring that was often noticeable. One female descendant's lips were described by a nurse to be as "dark as a bruise."

Because the trait is recessive, both parents would have to carry the gene for the "blue" skin in order for a child to be born with truly blue skin. However, it seems that even descendants with just one parent with the gene can also have more blue in their skin than the average person.

Out of the Blue

The intermarriage among the Fugates and some close relatives created a line of succession that resulted more than one hundred years later in the birth of Benjamin Stacy. Ben's blue skin was noticeable at birth, but soon turned into a skin tone of a normal Caucasian, which made doctors think Ben inherited the gene from only one parent.

Now at the age of twenty-five, Ben's "blue" coloring is barely noticeable. "I have friends that have known me for years without saying a word about my color," he says, noting that most of the bluish coloring is in his lips and fingernails. "My entire body is not blue, as some people seem to think." He says the slight shade of purple-blue coloring is more noticeable in his eyes and lips when the weather gets cooler, when he hasn't had enough sleep, or when he's sick. "The color of my lips and fingernails usually draws some attention," notes Ben, "but mostly out of curiosity or concern for my health. I have had no major health problems related to the disorder, and I simply try to live an average life in spite of being 'blue.'"

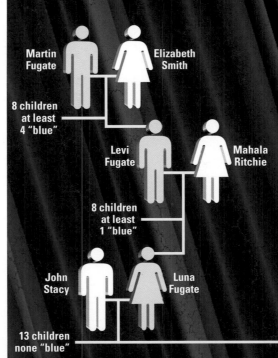

The Fugates of Troublesome Creek

Elizabeth and Martin Fugate passed on the gene for the blood disorder methemoglobinemia, which results in blue skin tones. The gene appears to have been passed down through the family for more than 150 years. Here is an abbreviated family tree, showing the link all the way down to the sixth generation, Ben Stacy.

Martin Fugate — Elizabeth Smith
8 children at least 4 "blue"
Levi Fugate — Mahala Ritchie
8 children at least 1 "blue"
John Stacy — Luna Fugate
13 children none "blue"
Bill Stacey — Mary Elizabeth Ritchie
Alva Stacey — Hilda B. Godsey
2 children 1 "blue"
Ben Stacey

INTERESTING TO NOTE: Mahala Ritchie's parents were Hannah Fugate and James Ritchie. Hilda Godsey's parents were Gladys Fugate and Paul Godsey. With such intermarrying between the same families, you can imagine how the descendants have kept the trait in their family for so long and how it was possible that both partners could have the gene for the blood disorder.

Activity

GENE JOURNALISM We can't look inside our ancestors to see where certain traits are from, but old family photos can provide strong clues. Decide if you want to study your own family (if family photos passed on for generations are available) or a celebrity family (autobiographies or biographies are often loaded with pictures of the famous person's grandparents, parents, children, etc.). After locating at least three generations of a family, write a family gene journal noting where each descendant probably got each trait. Besides obvious traits, try to note tiny details, such as the way their ears and eyebrows are shaped or even the places wrinkles formed on their faces. Does every person have some obvious traits from their parents?

AGAINST ALL ODDS

Genes determine almost everything about the way your body works, from the number of toes you have to whether you are male or female. When genes mutate—spontaneously change—they can be passed on to later generations. Many mutations cause diseases. If the gene is recessive, it may never show its consequences. But if by chance someone inherits two such recessive genes, that person may have a condition no one has ever heard of or seen. Before such genes were understood, their results were usually attributed to supernatural causes.

The X (left) and Y (below) chromosomes determine a person's gender. Females have two X chromosomes in their cells, while males have one X and one Y chromosome.

THE ELEPHANT MAN

London, England, 1862

John Merrick is born. When he is two years old, Merrick starts to develop growths on his face. By adolescence, huge, cauliflower-like tumors have covered his head and body. His right hand and forearm have become fused into a clublike appendage.

Merrick is an intelligent man, but no one will employ him because of his appearance. As a young man, he earns money selling shoe polish on the streets of London. He drags his misshapen feet when he walks, while children scream cruel insults at him. Before long, Merrick earns money a different way—he becomes a circus attraction. In sideshows, alongside sword swallowers and bearded ladies, he is exhibited as "the Elephant Man" because a growth on his face resembles a tusk. In 1890, his life comes to an end at Whitechapel Hospital.

Merrick himself believed that an elephant had frightened his mother just before he was born. This fright, he thought, had caused his physical deformities. A circus promoter claimed that his mother was trampled by an elephant while John was still in her womb. At this time, you'll recall, almost nothing was understood about genes—especially the inheritance of rare genes or mutations. The disease that afflicted Merrick is known as Proteus syndrome. Only ninety cases have ever been recorded.

The Complicated Case of the "Vampire" Gene

Is it possible that "vampires" walk on Earth? Canadian biochemist David Dolphin proposed that the people known as vampires might have really suffered from congenital erythropoietic porphyria. Only about two hundred cases of this illness have ever been recorded. Although the gene that causes it is extremely rare, the disorder could have become more common through marriage between relatives in some isolated communities.

Congenital erythropoietic porphyria is the rarest form of porphyria, which interferes with the production of heme. Heme is a key component of the blood's hemoglobin, the protein that carries oxygen throughout the body. Porphyria can have numerous effects on the body, especially in the skin and liver. Among its effects is a sensitivity to light. Exposure to the Sun can cause red sores and growths on a person's body. People with this ailment prefer nighttime—to avoid sunlight. The disorder causes the teeth to become reddish-brown, which may look like bloodstains. This rare porphyria creates ulcers that destroy the victim's cartilage and bone—the nose, ears, and fingers become deformed. A person might develop pointed ears, a flattened nose, and long fingers. Porphyria causes people to behave in strange ways. They have hallucinations and wild mood swings. King George III of England was said to have a form of porphyria, explaining the extreme pains and wild behavior he sometimes showed.

When he introduced his theory, Dolphin also claimed that chemicals in garlic—healthy for most people—would make the condition worse. This hasn't been proven, and it is not widely believed among scientists. Also, fear of vampires was so widespread in the eighteenth century that bodies believed to be "undead" were occasionally dug up, and they typically weren't disfigured, as his theory suggests. (And, yes, they were dead.) Finally, drinking blood from other people wouldn't help the condition.

It's also unlikely that the famous Count Vlad Dracula had the ailment. Perhaps porphyria symptoms got mixed up with stories about this cruel Romanian nobleman, who had his enemies impaled. We'll probably never know if vampire myths were really inspired by individuals with congenital erythropoietic porphyria or not. Even if "vampires" do exist, don't worry—porphyria is a genetic disorder, which means that there is no way you could get it from being bitten. (A disease you can catch from another person is known as an infectious disease.)

Activity

EXPERT OPINION Imagine you are a genetics specialist, and you are sent to a remote town where one of the inhabitants is afflicted with a genetic condition such as porphyria or Proteus syndrome. The frightened townspeople are susceptible to rumors and superstitions that this person is not human but a monster of some kind. You have called a town meeting to explain the medical facts so as to put the town's fears to rest. Based on what you know about gene mutation, write your speech to the town and share it with your class.

Stalking a Deadly Gene

Sometimes you have to give a little skin to get your job done—but it can be worth it. That's what Nancy Wexler had to do. Wexler is a psychologist at Columbia University in New York City. She's also traveled thousands of miles to solve a genetic puzzle: the secret of Huntington's disease, an inherited disorder. Unlike most genetic research, this particular quest is personal. Huntington's disease claimed the lives of Nancy Wexler's mother, three uncles, and a grandfather. Wexler knew that she had a fifty-fifty chance of developing the illness.

Decoding the Disease

Huntington's disease (HD) is a cruel, debilitating disease. Its sufferers lose control of their muscles so they may not be able to move easily. They may shake and jerk. They forget how to do even the simplest things. Because they lose their sense of balance, they may fall down and hurt themselves. They lose the ability to swallow and speak and so run a high risk of choking or starving.

In the 1970s, there was no way for doctors to predict who might get HD. People are born with it in their genes, but it doesn't usually begins causing symptoms until after the carrier is age thirty-five. By this time, the defective gene has often been passed on to the next generation.

Wexler wanted to find the gene for the illness, and her work was very important in identifying the gene. Her research led her to a village in Venezuela. A local doctor had written that many people in the village appeared drunk all the time. He said they couldn't control the way they moved and had slurred speech. Then the doctor talked to several villagers and decided that they were suffering from HD. The gene for the disease must have been very common in the local population.

Villagers knew that they had a disorder, but they were unfamiliar with research medicine. They didn't understand why Wexler had come, or why she wanted to take blood and skin samples from

them. Finally, Wexler convinced them by donating a sample of her own skin to show how it was done. Over a period of years, she convinced thousands of people to give her blood and skin samples.

Mutation Discovery

In 1983, Dr. James Guselle and a team of researchers at Massachusetts General Hospital used Wexler's collection of blood samples to begin the process toward finding the gene for HD. Using special enzymes to "cut" DNA strands, they analyzed

samples from families in which HD had appeared. They traced the family trees and eventually found a fragment of DNA linked with the affected members. It was located on chromosome 4. Ten years later, Guselle found the actual gene—the sequence of DNA that didn't work right—just where he expected it.

Further research identified the exact alteration or mutation in the HD gene that causes the disease. Now people can be tested to find out whether they have the defective gene before symptoms appear. About four thousand diseases are currently thought to be caused by genes, including some kinds of cancer, Alzheimer's disease, sickle-cell anemia, and cystic fibrosis.

Knowing what gene causes an illness won't cure it immediately. But it's a huge leap forward, because scientists can find out what defect the disease gene has and try to correct it. Wexler calls her work in tracking down the cause of HD "the most fantastic detective story in the entire world."

Maybe it's in your genes?

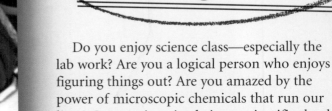

Do you enjoy science class—especially the lab work? Are you a logical person who enjoys figuring things out? Are you amazed by the power of microscopic chemicals that run our lives? Can you imagine being a scientific sleuth and solving genetic mysteries? Then, we've got the perfect job for you: genetic researcher. To become a genetic researcher, you'll need a college degree with a science major. Generally, it's necessary to have a master's or doctor's degree in some branch of biology. You'll need a lot of patience and curiosity, but think of all the important work you'll be doing.

Activity

QUIZ THE GENETICIST Invite a genetic researcher or a genetic counselor to your class to discuss recent genetic research and tests to screen inherited genetic disorders. Prepare a list of questions to ask before the scientist talks to the class.

Chromosome Comparison

You probably think you're nothing like other kids in your class. Guess again. Scientists estimate that 99.9% of the DNA of most humans is identical. Your genetic differences in physical appearance, behavior, or biochemistry (such as a tendency for a particular illness) account for only 1/1000th of your DNA. In fact, chimps and humans are about 98 percent identical genetically. We're cousins under the fur.

There may be more chances for genetic variation the more DNA an organism has. Mosquitoes, for example, seem really alike with only six chromosomes. But what do you think it means that a person has fewer chromosomes than an armadillo or a potato?

ORGANISM	NUMBER OF CHROMOSOMES
Corn	20
Pea	14
Apple	34
Onion	16
Potato	48
Cat	38
Dog	78
Goldfish	94
Horse	64
Human	46
Mosquito	6
Camel	70
Squirrel	40
Chimpanzee	48
Housefly	12
Fruit fly	8
Alligator	32
Chicken	78
Porpoise	44
Armadillo	64

Historic DNA

DNA can tell us quite a bit about our past. Comparing our genes to those of our ancestors may tell us how human beings evolved.

Compare Sequences. Nitrogen bases occur in DNA in particular sequences we call genes. Scientists can compare the sequence on a tiny sample of ancient DNA with the sequence on a sample of DNA from a living species to look for similarities or differences in the sequence.

Make Copies. Usually samples of DNA—a drop of blood, a hair, a fragment of brain tissue—are tiny and fragile. There is the danger that the DNA will be destroyed in the process of examining it. So scientists use a research tool called polymerase chain reaction (PCR). PCR allows scientists to make trillions of copies of a trace of DNA so that there is enough material to study.

Go for a Date. Scientists also use DNA dating. This method is based on how many mutations can be found in the DNA sample. Mutations occur over time, so by measuring how much human DNA has mutated from that of a sample, researchers can figure out how long it took for the mutations to occur. For example, scientists compared DNA discovered in the remains of a Neanderthal man with DNA found in humans today. They concluded that Neanderthals and modern humans had a common ancestor who lived between 550,000 and 690,000 years ago.

Gene Geography

The Human Genome Project, begun in 1990, is one of the largest scientific endeavors ever undertaken. Thirty-six countries have invested billions of dollars in the project for equipment, computers, scientists, and technicians. More than nine thousand scientists are trying to map the estimated thirty to forty thousand genes in human DNA. Human DNA has three billion chemical bases; a gene may be just a handful of them. The information scientists will collect could fill two thousand telephone books of five hundred pages each.

The gene map will show the location of every known gene. Only an estimated 3 percent of DNA contains protein-encoding genes, so just finding them is an effort beyond any previously known. Yet the project is ahead of schedule. Originally slated for a 2005 completion, the project should be finished in 2003. One of its main goals is to identify the location of disease-causing genes, so that one day, genetic engineering may allow scientists to repair human genes. The Human Genome Project might one day make these diseases and disorders a thing of the past.

Why just diseases and disorders? Well, some people might like to be able to turn their children into superhumans, "perfect" in every way. Most scientists, however, don't feel that is an appropriate way to use the Human Genome Project. They'd rather save their efforts for people who really need them.

How to Study DNA

- Take DNA from a specimen's cells.
- Mix DNA with a chemical that cuts it at particular sequences.
- Place fragments of DNA in a gel.
- Apply a shock of high-volt electricity.
- Short fragments move through gel quickly and fragments line up by size.
- Use a nylon membrane called a blot to lift fragments from gel.
- Treat the membrane with radioactive material. The radioactive material attaches to the DNA fragments.
- Take X-ray photos of the membrane.
- Pieces of DNA look like supermarket bar codes.
- Scientists can compare and analyze the dark bands on the X rays.

DESCRIPTION	GENE	CHROMOSOME
Alzheimer's disease, type 3	AD3	14
Alzheimer's disease, type 4	AD4	1
Amyotrophic lateral sclerosis	SOD1	21
Breast cancer, type 1	BRCA1	17
Breast cancer, type 2	BRCA2	13
Colon cancer, type 1	MSH2	2
Colon cancer, type 2	MLH1	3
Cystic fibrosis	CFTR	7
Gaucher disease	GBA	1
Juvenile onset diabetes	IDDM1	6 & 11
Malignant melanoma	CDKN2	9
Obesity	OBS	7
Phenylketonuria	PAH	12
X-linked mental retardation	FMR1	X

Juvenile Onset Diabetes

This disease is associated with changes in the DNA in an area on chromosome 6. Someone with these changes is more likely to develop IDDM. IDDM interferes with the body's ability to make and use insulin, a protein hormone essential to converting food to energy. Most diabetics have to take an injection of insulin on a regular basis. Risk of blindness, heart disease, kidney failure, nerve disorders, and other conditions can result from diabetes. It affects about sixteen million Americans. (Adult-onset diabetes, which generally affects people in middle age and later, also interferes with insulin production and has similar symptoms. Yet it stems from a different genetic cause.)

Here's a genetic puzzle: Why do some twins resemble each other almost exactly and others hardly at all? Genetics doesn't determine everything about us. Quite a bit can happen on the way.

Ordinarily, a woman's ovary releases just one egg per month into her uterus. If that egg is fertilized, it begins dividing again and again, constantly growing and doubling its number of cells. About nine months and trillions of cells later, an infant is born. Every once in a while—no one is exactly sure why—the ovary releases two eggs. Both eggs can be fertilized by separate sperm, and if they develop into children, they become fraternal twins. Another term for them is dizygotic twins, because they form from two zygotes (fertilized eggs). Since the egg and the sperm that went into the zygotes are different, fraternal twins are no more alike than any pair of siblings. Even their sex is different, as often as not. They are twins just because they are the same age—give or take a few minutes.

Once in a while, a single fertilized egg separates into two halves. Each half then begins dividing on its own and develops into two separate embryos. The resulting twins have the same chromosomes and DNA. The children of this twinning process are called monozygotic twins because they develop from one zygote ("mono" is a prefix from Greek meaning "one"). More than half of all identical twins are male. These twins usually look very, very much alike. Differences in lifestyles or events such as childhood injuries may affect their appearances, though. People who know a pair of identical twins can usually tell them apart.

Seventeen-year-old fraternal twins.

Nature and Nurture

Identical twins give scientists the unique opportunity to study the power of inheritance. Because twins are natural clones, or genetic copies, they have the same DNA. Countless studies have focused on monozygotic twins who were separated at birth and raised in different families. By studying these twins, scientists hope to discover what portion of our personalities, behaviors, and intelligence is controlled by genes, and how much is shaped by where, how, and with whom we live. There aren't very many such cases, however. Similarities between such twins can be eerie. Coincidence? Or genetic fate? Judge for yourself with the following stories.

Daphne and Barbara

Daphne Goodship and Barbara Herbert had not seen one another for thirty-nine years. When they first met, each woman wore a beige dress and a brown velvet jacket. Both had the annoying habit of pushing up their noses, which they called "squidging." At age sixteen, both had gone to dances where they met the men they later married. Each woman had two sons and one daughter.

Jack and Oscar

Jack Yufe and Oskar Stohr were twins born in Trinidad in 1933. After their parents divorced, Jack was raised in the Jewish faith. Oskar moved with his mother to Czechoslovakia and became a member of the Hitler Youth Nazi organization.

# of Twins

In 1979, the two met for the first time. At this meeting, each wore rectangular wire-rimmed glasses, short mustaches, and blue shirts with double pockets in the front. Instead of throwing away rubber bands, both men stored the bands on their wrists. And both liked to upset people by sneezing loudly in elevators.

The Two Jims

James Springer and Jim Lewis had been adopted into different families. Thirty-nine years later, they were brought together. Both had been named James. Each man had married and divorced a woman named Linda. Both had remarried women named Betty. Jim Lewis had named his firstborn son James Alan. Jim Springer had named his son James Allen. They both worked part time in law enforcement in the same county in Ohio.

Q: Do identical twins have the same fingerprints?

A: No, no one in the world has the exact same fingerprints! While identical twins may have the same set of genes, they usually develop differently. Identical genes will express themselves differently in different bodies, even in the same environment. Besides fingerprints, physical differences in identical twins may include height and weight.

Fantastic Facts on Twins

► Twins occur in about one out of ninety births.

► About one-third of all twins born are identical.

► About 18 to 22 percent of all twins are left-handed, while fewer than 10 percent of nontwins are left-handed.

► The word "twin" comes from an Old English word meaning "two together."

► Twins Days Festival is held in Twinsburg, Ohio, every August. In 1998, more than three thousand sets of twins attended, representing every state and more than a dozen countries.

► Fraternal twinning occurs in 2.4 percent of births.

► Between 1973 and 1990, twin births increased two times over the rate of single births. One of the main reasons for this is that many women are having children later in life and using fertility drugs. These drugs release more eggs, making it easier to become pregnant with twins.

Activity

PICTURE (ALMOST) PERFECT Find a picture of a family member or famous person who looks like you. Try to match up each facial feature to find your closest "twin." Do your eyebrows slant the same way? Did your teeth grow in similarly? Do you have almost identical hairstyles? How can you make yourself look different than your newfound "twin"?

Splitting Up Is Hard to Do

THREE WAYS TO PRODUCE TRIPLETS

❶ One sperm fertilizes one egg.

The fertilized egg divides into two eggs. One egg grows normally; the other divides again.

Result: identical triplets. They are always of the same sex.

❷ Two sperm fertilize two eggs.

One fertilized egg develops normally into an embryo. The other divides to form two eggs.

Result: triplets, two of whom are identical twins; the other is their fraternal sibling.

❸ Three sperm fertilize three separate eggs.

Result: fraternal triplets, all with different genetic makeup.

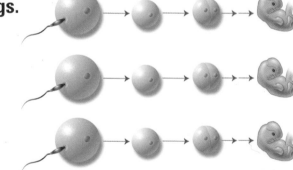

Ontario, Canada, 1934

The Dionne "Quints"

The Dionne children made history. Born in 1934, they were the first five identical babies, or quintuplets, to survive birth. At that time, scientists could not study the DNA of the quints, but the girls were almost certainly monozygotic siblings. Multiple births generally result from more than one zygote. Multiple births are much more common today because new fertility drugs sometimes make ovaries release several eggs in one month. In later years, the surviving Dionnes complained that as children they had been exploited by the government of Ontario, Canada, because of their uniqueness.

The Siamese Twins of North Carolina

Attached by a band of flesh that connected their livers, Chang and Eng Bunker were joined from their ribs down to about their navel. Such conjoined twins occur about once in every fifty thousand to eighty thousand births, when the developing embryos fail to separate. Today, doctors can often separate these infants with surgery. Chang and Eng changed the way people looked at others with physical differences. They held jobs, married, and raised families (a total of 22 children). Conjoined twins are often called "Siamese" twins in Chang and Eng's honor.

The celebrated Siamese twins, Chang and Eng, after traveling all the world and seeing the advantages and disadvantages of every country, chose the quiet glens of Wilkes as the loveliest spot for retirement and repose.

They were born in May 1811, at Maklong, Siam [now Thailand], and died in Wilkes county, near Hays post office, about the year 1880.

They were united together as one by an ensiform cartilage from the side. The blood vessels and nerves each communicated. There seemed to be a perfect sympathy, for when one was sick so was the other. They went to sleep at the same moment and woke at the same time. Both died the same day, only a few moments intervening between their deaths.

They were wealthy, well settled, and both happily married and had interesting families around them. They differed widely in appearance, character and strength. One was sober and patient; the other intemperate and irritable. It is said that they frequently fell out—generally about their movements—when they should or should not go somewhere—and sometimes fought like dogs. In 1870 Chang was stricken with paralysis from which he died a few years later. In a short time—probably about 30 minutes—Eng followed him to the great beyond. They were the most interesting persons that ever lived in the county. In the natural history of the world there is not another case like them.

—*excerpted from* HISTORICAL SKETCHES OF WILKES COUNTY, *Published by John Crouch in 1902*

Multiple Milestones

▶ On November 19, 1997, the world's first surviving septuplets were born—4 boys and 3 girls. They were born to a family in Carlisle, Iowa, a town of 3,400 people. They increased its population by 0.2%.

▶ The world's first set of octuplets was born on December 20, 1998—6 girls and 2 boys—in Austin, Texas. Altogether, the "octs" weighed in at about 10 pounds, one and one-half times the weight of a single, average baby.

Activity

MULTIPLES OF MULTIPLES One formula for predicting the number of multiple births goes like this: If one set of twins is born in every 90 live births, you can use this number to determine how many births there would have to be before triplets are produced. Simply multiply 90 by itself, and you get 8,100. When you multiply 90 x 90 x 90, you get the number of births for producing one set of quadruplets, and so on. Test this formula within your own community. Find out how many twins have been born in your local hospital in the past year, or count the number of twins in your school. Compare this number to the population of nontwins of the same age. Calculate how many babies would have to be born before triplets came along.

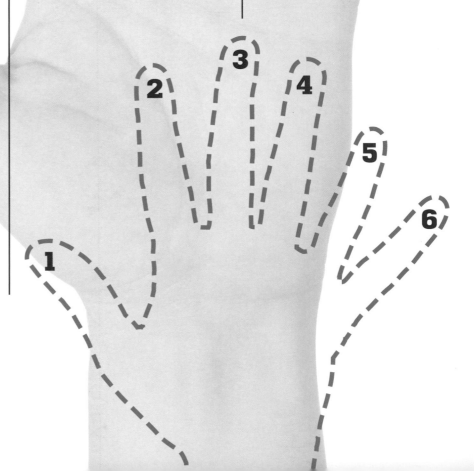

Give These

The rain pours down on this dreary, remote village. Three times you had to get out of the car to push a tire out of a rut, and your pants are caked with mud. But you're glad you've come. For a genetic sleuth, chasing a rare gene like the one for six fingers is worth the trouble. Supposedly, it behaves like neither a dominant nor a recessive gene, and you're determined to find out for sure. You're not sure how welcome you'll be, though. The villagers aren't used to strangers, and you don't know if they'll appreciate the scientific importance of what you're trying to do.

You stop on the outskirts of town and ask an elderly woman the way to a hotel. You notice her hands; they seem normal enough. Following her directions, you pull up at the village's one hotel. As you approach the door, a boy about twelve comes out. "Lemme help you with that," he says, reaching for your bag. You notice the boy has six fingers. An extra pinky on the outside of the hand fits at a slight angle to the rest of his fingers. The boy notices you looking and turns away. Better be a little more discreet in the future. You follow him into the hotel, where a woman about fifty years old is sweeping the front hall. She steps behind the counter and pulls out a guest book.

"How long will you be staying?" she asks.

"As long as it . . . oh, a few days."

"We don't get many travelers this time of year, with all the rain," she remarks. You can tell she's curious about you. Quickly you change the subject.

"Is that your son?"

She nods agreement. "Seems like a good kid," you say.

"Oh, Bill's a big help running this place. His sister is, too. My husband's on the fishing boat so much of the day. Oh, here he is now."

A man comes in. He nods toward you and gives his wife a peck on the cheek.

Quickly you glance at his hands: five fingers. Strange that neither of Bill's parents has six fingers. The hotelkeeper hands you a key.

"Jenny," she calls to someone upstairs, "make sure there are sheets on the bed in room 3." Then she directs you to a room at the top of the stairs.

People a Hand

A young woman of eighteen is coming out of the room. "All set," she remarks. She has the same features as Bill, but you count just five fingers.

"You must be the daughter of the house," you start out. "Nice to see a family all in business together."

"In a town like this, there are only a few businesses. I help out here and at my grandfather's store in the morning, when it's busier."

"What kind of store?" you inquire.

"General goods—groceries, medicine, shampoo, and the like. Fresh vegetables when we get them."

"Where's the store? It's too early for dinner, but I could use a snack."

"Up the street, make a left. If you're lucky, Grandpa will have doughnuts. He makes them there. They're the best."

You walk to the store. An old man sits on a chair inside. His hands are folded on one knee. Five fingers.

"I hear you have the best doughnuts in town," you say.

His face brightens. "You must be staying at the hotel. Yeah, I have a few left. They're this morning's, mind you. Come back for more tomorrow, when they're fresh."

You pick a bottle of juice out of the cooler to wash down the doughnuts. There's a large black-and-white photograph on the wall behind the proprietor; a man and woman sitting in front of their standing children. The woman's hand is on her husband's arm, and you can just make out an extra pinky. "Been in business here long?" you ask.

The man gives you a suspicious look, but he talks. "About ten years. I bought it from another fellow when I gave up farming. My hands couldn't take it."

"Farming's a tough life. Did you have an accident?"

He pauses, then lets out his breath. "My mother had an extra finger. The story was that her mother got scared by a wolf when she was in the womb, some nonsense like that."

"Her father had only five fingers?"

"That's right. No one around here had ever seen such a thing."

"But she passed it on to her children?"

"My older brothers were born with regular hands. But when I came out, my mother saw the extra finger and let out a shriek. She said it was a curse. A nuisance is what it was. She took me to a doctor who removed it." He held up the hand, where a small scar showed on the side. "Looks okay, but as I got older, the joint where the sixth finger used to be started to hurt a lot. When my son was born with the sixth finger, my mother advised me to do the same to him. He has three kids, and only one, the younger boy, has six fingers. Seems like one in every family."

Based on the evidence you've collected, is this gene dominant or recessive? A Punnett square will help you out. How did the six-fingered trait spread through the family? Make up a family tree and indicate the genotype of every member of the family with this trait. (Answers and explanations on page 32.)

Gene Splicing

History was made in 1973, when two scientists took a gene from the DNA of an African clawed frog and transplanted it into a bacterium. Their experiment created the first living cells that had DNA from one organism added to another's DNA. One common use of genetic engineering is to place a human gene into the DNA of *E. coli* bacteria. These engineered microorganisms then produce something, such as an antibody to fight infection, that we want. Here's a quick how-to for the technique of gene splicing.

1. A piece of human DNA is "snipped" from its chromosome using special chemicals.
2. Another gene is cut and the snipped section inserted into it, or spliced. The result is called recombinant DNA.
3. The recombinant DNA is injected into the cell nucleus of a bacterium such as *E. coli*. If the procedure is successful, that bacterium will pass the gene along to all its offspring, so a whole colony of genetically engineered bacteria can function as a little biological factory.

The Suicidal Spud

If you were to rank the benefits to the world brought by our knowledge of genetics, what would come in first? The potato with the self-destruct switch, of course.

This suicidal potato was created by geneticists—its enemy is a fungus. If the potato is attacked by the fungus, it sacrifices itself, taking the fungus with it. That way the fungus can't spread to the entire field of potatoes. Think about that next time you eat an order of fries.

Genetic engineers created this special potato by copying the fungus's gene for an enzyme called barnase. Then they placed that gene into the potato's DNA. If the potato is attacked by the fungus, its own gene kills it before the fungus can eat the potato and spread.

Uses of Genetic Engineering

▶ **Dairy farming:** Genetically engineered cows produce milk containing lactoferrin, a protein that fights harmful bacteria.

▶ **Drug manufacture:** The milk of altered sheep contains chemicals to fight lung disease, and goats can produce anticoagulants, chemicals that dissolve blood clots.

▶ **Medicine:** Drugs produced from genetic engineering have helped millions of people fight heart disease, cancer, AIDS, and strokes.

The Bean Gene

Genetic engineering can improve your life—and the lives of those around you. If you've ever had a large portion of chili, baked beans, or pasta fagiole, you know what we're talking about. The infamous "gas attacks" that give beans—an extremely healthy food, rich in protein and low in fat—a bad name occur because beans contain complex carbohydrates that most people have a hard time digesting. Genetic engineers are developing new kinds of beans that are more easily digestible.

Calling All Clones

A team of scientists at Texas A&M University are trying to clone Missy, the pet dog of a local couple. If the Missyplicity Project is successful, it will be the first cloning of a dog. So far, this project has cost about 2.3 million dollars.

That's nothing compared to the efforts of a group of Japanese scientists led by Kazufumi Goto. This group is looking to clone an animal that has been extinct for at least ten thousand years: a woolly mammoth. These hairy, tusked creatures roamed Earth during the last Ice Age.

The first thing you need to clone a cell is DNA. But cells decay after they die, and after ten thousand years, bones are all that remain. Goto and his colleagues hope to find preserved remains of a woolly mammoth in Siberia, in the frozen soil called permafrost, which never thaws.

Genetic material usually wastes away after the cells die, even in a frozen environment like Siberia's.

If Japanese researchers found a mature male mammoth with cells intact, they would place the nucleus of a cell into an egg of an elephant, then jolt it with electricity. The fertilized egg would be implanted into the uterus of an elephant. If the animals are related closely enough, the mammoth embryo would grow in the elephant's uterus. Six hundred days later, the first baby mammoth in ten thousand years would be born.

Shape of Things to Come

Easier on the stomach and easier on the packer. Fruits and vegetables come in the shapes that nature intended for them, not the shapes that fit best inside cardboard boxes. Much of the cost of fresh foods is in shipping, so a more efficient shape will offer a benefit to the pocketbook. But will people buy a square cabbage, or a straight banana?

HowBigIsYourDNA?

▶ The genome of a human consists of three billion bases.

▶ The nucleus of a single, microscopic cell holds more than 6 feet (1.8 meters) of DNA.

▶ If all the DNA in all the cells of a human being were stretched out in a line, it would reach to the Moon and back eight thousand times.

HOLLYWOOD CLONES

The movie *Jurassic Park*, based on a novel by Michael Crichton, explores what could happen if scientists were able to clone dinosaurs. In the movie, scientists use dinosaur genetic material they find in insect bodies that were preserved in the hardened sap of trees for millions of years. The cloned dinosaurs are placed in a theme park on an island. Naturally, havoc and destruction follow, but that's Hollywood!

Activity

GENES ARE FOR KEEPS "Altered" animals are bred with others in controlled situations, but if a recombinant gene escapes into the wild, a species of living thing may change forever. Hold a classroom debate about the benefits and drawbacks of genetic engineering. Is it right to change other organisms to help humans? If you were a genetic engineer, what might be some things you might try to improve or change through genetic engineering methods?

Final Project:
All in the Family

"He has his mother's eyes." Have you ever heard that or something like it? Genes run in families. By studying inheritance patterns of your own family, you can do science firsthand.

Make detailed observations of physical traits of as many relatives as possible—include parents, siblings, grandparents, aunts, uncles, and cousins. A list of traits below is a starting point, but you can add more if you want. Bear in mind that many traits, such as eye color, complexion, and height, are determined by more than one gene.

Use your collected information to make a family tree showing how one or more traits have been passed down through the family. Then, compile the information into a table like the one here, adding any other traits you've recorded. Compare this information with that collected by other students. Are the comparisons similar or different?

ANSWERS

Solve-It-Yourself Mystery, pages 28–29:
Bill's great-grandmother had a genetic mutation that gave her six fingers. Some of her children had five fingers, and one had six. Since this was the first case of six fingers seen in the town, you can assume that her husband had only genes for five fingers. If it was recessive, none of the children would have shown the trait, so it must have been dominant. Bill's grandfather and father both had the extra finger removed, so they had the gene even though they didn't appear to. A Punnett square for the gene would look like this:

	f	f
F	Ff	Ff
f	ff	ff

F stands for the dominant six-fingered gene; f stands for the normal five fingers. The genotype for the six-fingered parent is on the left; the five-fingered parent is on top.

TRAIT	PERCENT OF FAMILY MEMBERS	DOMINANT OR RECESSIVE	GENOTYPE
Dimples			
Cleft Chin			
Attached earlobes			
Widow's peak			
Hair on fingers			
Freckles			